A BOOK
OF THEIR OWN

by Barbara A. Donovan
illustrated by Dana Regan

Scott Foresman
is an imprint of

Glenview, Illinois • Boston, Massachusetts • Mesa, Arizona
Shoreview, Minnesota • Upper Saddle River, New Jersey

Illustrator CVR, 4, 7, 9, 12, 15, 18, 21, 23 Dana Regan

Photographs
Every effort has been made to secure permission and provide appropriate credit for photographic material. The publisher deeply regrets any omission and pledges to correct errors called to its attention in subsequent editions.

Unless otherwise acknowledged, all photographs are the property of Pearson Education, Inc.

24 © Paul Rapson/Alamy Images

4 5 6 7 8 9 10 V0N4 13 12 11 10

CONTENTS

3

Chapter 1 ❈ The Library Book

To Toni Vasquez, the ticking library clock was a constant reminder that she'd procrastinated for too long, and now she and her research assignment were in big trouble. Seven books lay open on the table in front of her. Ragged slips of paper spilled from each one to remind her where to find key information for her report. With a frustrated groan, Toni put her face in her hands. *How will I ever finish recording all these notes, let alone write this report before tomorrow?*

Toni forced herself to breathe deeply and focus, the way her mother had taught her whenever she felt anxious and overwhelmed. *Take two minutes,* her mother would advise. *Sort out what must be done, and then decide what is most important.*

I have to write the report, or I risk failing Social Studies, Toni admitted to herself. *First I need to focus on the part of each book that has the information I need.*

Toni closed her eyes to think. *Taking notes takes too much time. How can I speed up this process?*

A solution seeped into Toni's mind, but she quickly ignored it because she knew it was wrong. The ticking clock counted off the seconds she could ill afford to lose. Once again the solution to her problem crept into her thoughts. But before she could shove it aside once again, Toni began to think up reasons to excuse her behavior.

If I only use pencil, I can go back later and fix it, Toni said to herself. *I'll save so much time. I'll be able to finish my report and get a good grade, which will make everyone happy. And besides that, no one will ever know.*

Like a criminal checking for witnesses, Toni casually gazed around at the other students working at the tables scattered around the library. No one seemed aware of her presence. A line of children checking out books kept Mrs. Jackson, the librarian, distracted. The coast was clear; it was now or never.

Gingerly, Toni lifted her pencil from the scarred wooden table. With another quick look, she made a final check of the people around her. Then Toni set to work underlining the facts she needed in the library book in front of her. Minutes passed with no one noticing her.

Just as Toni was finishing with her first book, she sensed that someone was approaching. Quickly, she closed that book and opened another. Pretending to be engaged in the book, Toni didn't look up when a pair of black pants came into view. When it was clear that Mrs. Jackson wasn't moving, Toni lifted her eyes and met the librarian's disappointed stare.

A blush lit Toni's face with shame as the librarian slid into the seat beside her and retrieved the book Toni had just closed. As Toni started to spout her excuses, Mrs. Jackson simply held up her hand. "I think you know that what you did was wrong."

Toni hung her head as Mrs. Jackson spoke quietly, "I could ban you from the library for this," she continued as Toni's shocked eyes met hers. "I imagine that will make it very difficult for you to complete school assignments. I trust you don't want that to happen?"

"No, Mrs. Jackson," Toni said tearfully. "That would be awful. I promise it won't happen again."

"I hope not, Toni, which is why I'll make a deal with you."

"Anything, Mrs. Jackson. Anything," Toni pleaded.

"Meet me here at 9:00 a.m. sharp for the next three Saturdays. You and I will work together repairing books that people have torn, written in, or otherwise damaged."

As she returned to her desk, Mrs. Jackson held up the book Toni had been using. "I think we'll start with this one."

Toni spent the next two hours diligently taking notes at the library. She knew that looking for any more shortcuts was simply out of the question. The report would probably take all night to finish, but she was determined to get it done on time.

Around midnight, Toni put the final touches on the report and collapsed into bed—promising herself that she would *never* leave things to the last minute again.

Chapter 2 ❈ A Book of My Own

The following Saturday at 8:55 in the morning, Toni locked her bike in the rack behind the library. Sadly, she waved to her friends as they sped off to the park. Toni trudged up the stairs and pulled on the glass doors, but they didn't budge. Toni cupped her hands and peered inside. She could see Mrs. Jackson seated behind her desk. Toni rapped lightly on the glass, and Mrs. Jackson glanced up and smiled.

As she rose from her desk, Mrs. Jackson removed a green coil with keys on it from her wrist. She unlocked the door and held it open as Toni slipped inside. Mrs. Jackson relocked the door. "Good. You're early," she said pleasantly. "The library doesn't open for another hour, so we'll have peace and quiet while we work."

Toni breathed a sigh of relief. She'd anticipated a scolding, but instead Mrs. Jackson led her to an old worktable tucked between the main desk and the stacks of encyclopedias. On the desk was a box filled with books, some white erasers, two brushes, some tape, paper towels, and a small box of assorted tools.

Mrs. Jackson sat beside Toni as she explained the process they would use to repair the books. "Your job will be to go through this book page by page and erase any pencil marks you see." She held out the book Toni had marked up, and with a guilty nod, Toni accepted it. Then Mrs. Jackson gave Toni one of the white erasers and a brush.

"This is a special kind of eraser that won't smear the pencil marks or the print on the page. Always rub the eraser in one direction—towards the edge of the page—not back and forth. As you finish a page, use the brush to carefully remove all the eraser dust and any other debris from the page. Check for any loose pages, or ones that have rips, grease, food, or other stains on them. Write those page numbers on this sheet of paper and stick it in the book. I'll fix those things when you're done with your part of the job. OK?"

Toni nodded, and the two of them began working in a comfortable silence. Before long, Toni came across a page on which someone had written notes in ink in the margin. "Will this eraser work on ink too, Mrs. Jackson?" Toni asked as she held out the book for the librarian's review.

Mrs. Jackson sighed as she gently clasped the book in her hands. "No, Toni, it won't. If someone uses ink or marker, we can't do anything to fix it." She shook her head and said, "This makes me so sad." After a minute, she went on. "When I was young, my family didn't have a lot of money. Owning a book was a luxury that was as far from my reach as the moon. But once every month or so, a mobile library rolled into our little town. For a reader like me, that mobile library was a treasure chest. I got chills each time I walked up the steps of that old blue bus and saw row after row of books. Because there were so many people who wanted to take out books, we could only check out one book at a time."

A faraway smile curled Mrs. Jackson's lips as she remembered. "Oh, I took my time choosing that one special book to read each time. Then I would read that book over and over again until the mobile library came back into town."

Mrs. Jackson's tales of her love of books fascinated Toni. At last Toni asked, "Did you ever get a book of your own when you were a child?"

"Actually, Toni, I did," answered Mrs. Jackson. "One day when I was about nine years old, this grand lady came into our classroom. I'll never forget her. She had on this swirling black cape that dusted her shoes and a red felt hat with a purple feather so long that it practically touched her back. In her hands were two bulging shopping bags. The lady's eyes gleamed as she told us that she had brought a present for each and every student. Can you guess what those presents were?" she asked Toni.

"Books!" exclaimed Toni.

"Exactly! Books!" cried Mrs. Jackson. "You have no idea how much a book of our own meant to my friends and me. I'll bet I read my book from cover to cover a thousand times. Sometimes we would trade books, but never for long. Our books were precious to us, and we didn't want anything to happen to them."

Chapter 3 ❀ A Book of Their Own

Her time with Mrs. Jackson gave Toni a lot to think about over the next week. At 9:00 the next Saturday morning, Toni eagerly knocked on the library's glass doors. She slid under the librarian's arm as she entered the cool silence of the library. Toni said, "I have something for you, Mrs. Jackson. Well, it's not exactly for you. Anyway, I'll show you."

When they reached their worktable, Toni dug deep into each pocket of her jeans. Crumpled dollar bills and several coins spilled onto the table. A puzzled look crossed Mrs. Jackson's face as the pile grew.

"Here," said Toni as she shoved the money toward Mrs. Jackson. "I want to buy a book for a child who doesn't have one."

Mrs. Jackson was stunned. She had no idea that her story would have such an effect on Toni. As they worked together that day, they discussed the kinds of books Toni liked to read. Mrs. Jackson shared with Toni the books she'd liked as a young girl too. Together, they decided on the perfect book for Toni to buy for another child. And Mrs. Jackson said she knew just the girl who would appreciate it.

When Toni returned the next week with more money for more books, Mrs. Jackson asked Toni where the money was coming from.

"Buying a book for someone who has never owned one before made me really happy. So I decided to buy more books for more children," Toni stated. Then she grabbed a book and an eraser and began scanning the book for marks. "When I left here last Saturday, I washed my mom's car. Then I walked Mr. Kelly's two dogs. Every chance I got this week, I found ways to earn money for books."

"Are you sure this is how you want to spend your money?" Mrs. Jackson asked kindly. "You're being very generous. Shouldn't you be saving your money for something you want?"

"Right now, there's nothing I want more than to give books to children who don't have any. Is that wrong?" Toni asked.

"No, Toni, there's nothing wrong with that. Now let's think about what book we should buy next."

As Toni completed her third week of work, she and Mrs. Jackson settled on a new title to buy. The librarian assured Toni that she knew just the child who would love to dive into that book.

When they said their good-byes, Mrs. Jackson did not expect to see Toni again the next Saturday, but she did. And this time Toni brought her two best friends, Vanessa and Sandy.

"What a surprise!" Mrs. Jackson said as she unlocked the library's doors for the girls. "To what do I owe the pleasure of this visit? You haven't marked up any more books, have you, Toni?"

Toni blushed and insisted, "Of course not!" Then she held out a paper bag to Mrs. Jackson. Inside the bag was a coffee can filled with money.

"What's all this money for?" Mrs. Jackson asked.

Vanessa stepped up and said, "Sandy and I found out about the books that you helped Toni buy for some children. Since we all love to read, we decided we wanted to help. So we ran errands and did other jobs this week to raise money for more books. Do you know of any other children who would like books of their own?" Vanessa asked.

"Will you help us, please?" asked Sandy. "We really want to chip in."

Mrs. Jackson looked from one hopeful face to the next. "You are all amazing. Of course, I'll help you. Do you have any ideas about the books you want to buy?"

The three girls pulled some chairs up to the worktable. Toni showed her friends how to repair the books. Then the three girls set to work as they chatted with Mrs. Jackson about possible titles to buy.

Chapter 4 ❀ A Hometown Hero

It didn't take long for news of Toni's "A Book of Their Own" project to spread around her school. Toni, Vanessa, and Sandy spent much of each recess talking to their classmates who had lots of questions. They wanted to know why the three girls were doing odd jobs instead of playing on the weekends.

One day after school, Toni, Vanessa, and Sandy sat on the swings at the park. Toni said, "Most of the kids I've talked to want to help. The problem is that they don't have time to earn extra money for books." Toni gently pushed off and swung in a low curve above the ground. "How can they help out?"

Ideas popped like popcorn from their heads, and they giggled at some of the crazy plans they came up with. Then Sandy said something that made the girls stop swinging. They talked excitedly about Sandy's idea, and within minutes they were soaring on their swings. Problem solved!

Well, not exactly solved yet. First, Toni and her friends had to talk to Mr. Hanover, the school principal. Mr. Hanover had heard about Toni's project and had called Mrs. Jackson to ask about it. He was interested in doing what he could to help.

"We want to have a toy sale," Toni explained to Mr. Hanover. "We all have toys at home that are still in good condition but that we don't play with anymore. Our idea is to donate these toys to the toy sale. People can buy them, and then we will use the money to buy books for children who otherwise couldn't afford them."

Mr. Hanover, who always encouraged his students to be considerate of others, approved of Toni's plan. On the day of the big toy sale, Toni was surprised when Mr. Hanover approached her accompanied by a young man with a camera slung around his neck.

"This is Nate Long," the principal said. "He's a writer for *The Town Crier,* and he'd like to write a story about "A Book of Their Own.""

Embarrassed, but pleased, Toni smiled for the camera and explained how making a big mistake had led her to do something to help others. She answered each of the reporter's questions and made sure that he took pictures of Vanessa and Sandy too. He also snapped a shot of Mrs. Jackson, who was helping out with the toy sale.

But when the reporter asked, "How does it feel to be a local hero?" Toni was shocked.

"Me? I'm not a hero," she stammered. "People like police officers and firefighters are heroes. I'm no hero. All I want to do is raise money for children who haven't had a chance to own books of their own."

When the story ran in the newspaper, the telephone at Toni's house didn't stop ringing for days. Friends, neighbors, uncles, aunts—you name it—everyone called to tell Toni how wonderful they thought her idea was. Everyone wanted to send money to buy more books for children. Even people Toni didn't know, but who had read the newspaper story, sent letters with money for books.

The next Saturday morning, Toni and Mrs. Jackson sat at the worktable to read the letters people had sent to Toni. Many letters included stories about why they wanted to help Toni's book drive. Some told of favorite books they had owned. Others told how they, like Mrs. Jackson, had always wanted a book but couldn't afford to own one.

Toni couldn't believe how her little idea had blossomed. She hadn't started out to be a hero. All she wanted was to help one child own a book. To that one child, Toni guessed, she was a hero after all.

Books on Wheels

Not all communities have library buildings. Some communities depend on buses or vans to bring books to residents. These vans are called mobile libraries. Some mobile libraries visit young children in day care centers. Others visit the elderly at senior centers. Some even go to people's homes if they cannot get to the library because of illness or other reasons.

Today's mobile libraries contain more than books. Some have computers. In a mobile library, people can check out books, do research on the Internet, and even order books from other libraries.